This book belongs to:

....

For Caleb and Rick xx

The Snot that he Forgot

Written by Leonie Lodge
Illustrations by Hend Moharram

Stanley's nose was always full of snot,
Everyone called it "The Snot that he forgot."

It was yellow and icky
and drippy like a tap,
Sometimes he'd squish it, roll it,
flick it and watch it go...

Splat

It seems that snotty Stanley
had a bit of an issue,
And all his mum wanted was
for him to use a tissue.

No matter where he went
his nose was always running,
And that's just what he'd do
when he saw his mum coming.

He'd **spin**

He'd **skip**

He'd **jump**

so she couldn't wipe his nose,
But she just wanted to stop it from
dripping on his toes!

She'd stuff tissues in his pockets
and up his sleeves,
In his socks, even under his hat
would you believe?!

Getting undressed at bedtime,
tissues flew out from his
sleeves into the bath,

SWHOOSH

Mixing with water
and leaving a slushy
aftermath.

The slush in the bath was not the end of Stanley's troubles,

You'll never guess what happened to his pet dog Mr McBubbles!

Stanley's dad got him a place in
the *Dazzling Dog Contest*,
The family were excited because
he really was the best.
But friendly Mr McBubbles
loved licking Stanley's nose.....

So he caught the flu and was too tired
to stand, let alone prance and pose.

Mr McBubbles missed the competition
and the whole family were upset,
But Stanley still wouldn't wipe his nose,
so there were more disasters yet.

There was the day that Stanley raided
the biscuit tin,
He wandered over, checked the door and
put his hand straight in.

But Stanley had rubbed his
snotty nose and hadn't
washed his hands, so
blaming his little sister was
not the best of plans.

His mum had seen the glistening snot on the blue tin lid, so although she didn't catch him she knew exactly what he did!

A few weeks later for Stanley's birthday
he had a little party,
His friends came — Oscar, Sophia, Noah,
Luna and his best friend, Marty.
They all sang HAPPY BIRTHDAY
And waited for Stanley to blow but.....

"AAAAATCHOO"

Bubble

Splat

"NOOOOOOOO"

Stanley let out the biggest sneeze you ever
did hear,
Then a bubble of snot
the size of a tennis ball appeared.

Oh yes the **Splat** landed
all over his perfect birthday cake,
The boys and girls were sad
because there was none for them to take.

The following week Stanley's friends came back for a cake with chocolate flakes, Stanley was really lucky because his mum loved to bake.

The kids were fed and happy and Stanley's nose was actually clear,
He FINALLY sneezed into a tissue,

"A-A-AAAATCHOOOOOO"

And everybody cheered!

Remember kids,
Clean noses
Happy poses!

Printed in Great Britain
by Amazon